Other Books by Heather Day Gilbert:

Out of Circulation, Book One in the *Hemlock Creek Suspense* Series

Miranda Warning, Book One in *A Murder in the Mountains* Series

Trial by Twelve, Book Two in *A Murder in the Mountains* Series

God's Daughter, Book One in the *Vikings of the New World Saga*

Forest Child, Book Two in the *Vikings of the New World Saga*

The Message in a Bottle Romance Collection

Praise for Indie Publishing Handbook: Four Key Elements for the Self-Publisher:

"Heather Day Gilbert is a teacher, encourager and fellow sojourner, with an extraordinary heart to help authors wade through this new world of publishing. Her newest release, *Indie Publishing Handbook: Four Key Elements for the Self-Publisher,* is a product of that genuine spirit. Written in the most relatable language, this book will inform and inspire you to finally take the leap into publishing independently."

~**Connie Almony,** author of Amazon Bestseller *At the Edge of a Dark Forest*

"Whether you've decided to jump head first into the self-publishing pool, or are still in the should-I-or-shouldn't-I phase, the *Indie Publishing Handbook* is required reading. Heather Day Gilbert lays out four essentials that every wannabe indie author should know, all written in a straightforward, easy to understand format. Highly recommended."

~**Michelle Griep,** author of *Writer Off the Leash: Growing in the Writing Craft*

"Don't be fooled by the size of this handbook. It's a goldmine of information for both new and established indie authors. If you can buy only one guide to indie publishing, make it this one."

~**Karin Kaufman**, author of *The Witch Tree*, a 2011 Grace Awards Finalist

"Concise, practical guidance from a novelist who has learned to negotiate the obstacles and opportunities of becoming your own publisher."

~**Andy Scheer**, book editor and writing coach

INDIE PUBLISHING HANDBOOK:

Four Key Elements for the Self-Publisher

Heather Day Gilbert

Indie Publishing Handbook:
Four Key Elements for the Self-Publisher
By Heather Day Gilbert

Copyright 2014 Heather Day Gilbert
Updated 2017

Cover Design by James, GoOnWrite.com
Interior Formatting by Polgarus Studio

Published by WoodHaven Press

All rights reserved. No part of this publication may be reproduced in any form, stored in any retrieval system, posted on any website, or transmitted in any form or by any means, without written permission from the publisher, except for brief quotations in printed reviews and articles.

Author Information: http://www.heatherdaygilbert.com
Author Newsletter: http://eepurl.com/Q6w6X

To all the diligent, undiscovered authors who have been told "no," but still believe they have a story to share

Contents

Introduction 1

Chapter One:
The Four Elements of Indie Publishing 5

Chapter Two:
Don't Rush the Process—Edit First! 7

Chapter Three:
The Fun Part—Developing Cover Art and
a Killer Blurb 19

Chapter Four:
The Tedious Part—Formatting and
Uploading your Book 25

Chapter Five:
The Never-Ending Story— Marketing your Novel 31

Wrap-Up and My Author Biography 43

Bonus: Wise Words from Multi-Published
Indie Authors 47

Acknowledgments 53

Introduction

Because I've been asked numerous times by author friends regarding what's involved in becoming an indie (independent) author, I wanted to write a simple guidebook that covers four key elements of indie publishing.

I've indie published six books, and I have two more scheduled for publication in 2017. You can read more about my "street cred" in my biography in the final chapter.

Keep in mind there are numerous ever-changing details involved in indie publishing (how to upload your book, where to upload, distribution, etc.). I'm not going to tackle the ins and outs of everything in this handbook. To be honest, the best place to find recent information and stay up-to-date is *not* in an e-book, but on blogs such as *The Creative Penn* or *The Book Designer*, or with online indie author groups.

But this little handbook will give you an overview of what's involved in the indie publication process so you can make an informed decision if indie publishing is right for you. I'll focus on four key elements the independent publisher has to handle/oversee. How you handle these elements is up to you, based on your monetary and time constraints.

For the purposes of this handbook, I'll share what I did to launch my books, but understand that the beauty of indie publishing is that you can pick and choose what methods you want to use. Therefore, this guidebook isn't prescriptive in the least. I'll just share what I did. But the *four key elements* don't change. You will need to be prepared to oversee them, outsource them, or learn how to effectively *do them yourself* to indie publish.

One more thing: before you begin any of this process, you will want to develop a social media platform. Yes, I understand it's hard to build one with no book to offer.

But act as if you're an author going somewhere. Get author pictures taken by someone who can make you look your best. Start a website/blog *in your name* (for easier discoverability by future readers), and be sure to use one of those author shots there. Start a Facebook author page. Create a Twitter account. Add Pinterest, Instagram, whatever you think your readers will migrate to (again, using your author name for all these venues will save time renaming when you have books out). Feel free to focus only on platforms you feel comfortable with, but *try* more than you think you will like. I held off on Twitter and Pinterest, only to later discover they are some of my most effective marketing tools.

I started blogging in the days when blogs were huge. They're not so important now, but it is crucial to have a *home base* (website) where readers can find you once you have a book to sell. Think of where you go online when you discover a new author. To his/her Facebook page? Blog? Twitter? That is exactly where your readers will be looking to find you.

One easy way to ease into blogging is to interview authors in your genre. Offer book giveaways. Interviewing fellow authors builds rapport and friendships, which is something that will be invaluable to you in this indie journey.

Finally, be careful about the blog platform and theme you choose. If you go with a free theme, be sure it has enough widget and plug-in capability to showcase your books and highlight your social media links. I had to change my blog theme once I had books out, because although the one I'd chosen was pretty, it had practically no widget capabilities. It is far easier to start out with a highly-functioning blog or theme than to import all your blog posts and revamp at a later date.

Chapter One:
The Four Elements of Indie Publishing

The very definition of indie publishing is that you are in charge of all aspects of your book's publication…from cover art to formatting, from edits to uploading. In fact, I would say there are **four** key elements indie authors control when publishing their books. By *control*, I mean you are the overseer—you can outsource it or learn to do it yourself. But the goal is to bring a competitive book to your readers, so you want to use the best you can afford or learn to *be* the best in these four aspects.

The **Four Elements** are:

Editing

Cover Art/Book Blurb

Formatting/Uploading

Marketing

Since I am familiar with fiction, this book will focus on publishing your first indie novel. However, I do believe non-fiction and even children's fiction authors will be able to take away ideas from this little handbook.

Keep in mind that the biggest expense for the indie author seeking to produce an outstanding book is **time.** Uploading your book to various vendors, such as Amazon, Nook, or iBooks, costs nothing. Having CreateSpace print and distribute your softcovers costs you nothing. You can spend as much or as little as you please on the four aspects mentioned above. But time is something the indie author must be prepared to invest.

Chapter Two:
Don't Rush the Process—Edit First!

A key part of the indie publication process is having editorial eyes on your manuscript—making sure it has been refined (even as if by fire) before you publish it. In this chapter, we will cover various forms of edits you can choose to run your manuscript through.

Why are edits important? Your debut novel will be something you can either *refer readers to* or *try to hide from* in the future. Yes, you can update your online books at any time. But if you publish softcovers, those are out in the world once you sell them or give them away to readers.

Besides, just like giving birth to your first child, why not do everything you can to make sure your book "baby" emerges into the reader world safe and sound? This debut novel is your résumé. So you want to give it one hundred percent.

There are a variety of eyes you can have on that manuscript, such as:

Critique Partners or Critique Groups

Beta Readers

Editors

Early Readers

I will briefly elaborate on the importance of these readers. **I would highly encourage you to run your novel through at least *three* of these critique stages**. Keep in mind, all these options are free *except* editors (unless you can barter services for a free edit).

Critique partner/critique group: These are people (readers or authors) who will read your rough drafts. They will stop a bad story in its tracks. They will ask uncomfortable questions and suggest possible changes to your characters or plot. They will pull you up short if you are writing in the wrong genre and it's not working. In other words, they will save you from making an idiot of yourself and writing a sub-par book.

I have one special critique partner, and she is also an author. Her style of writing is not the same as mine—we complement each other. Where I am weak, she is strong, and vice versa. We are totally honest if a story idea sounds dull, a genre doesn't seem like it's working, or characters/plot fall flat.

I have also participated in an online critique group in one of my genres (historical fiction). This group had varying levels of talent and did demand a large chunk of my time in return (we critiqued three separate chapters for three critiques on one of our own chapters). One thing I learned: listen to those who have already been published. You might not agree with what they say, but they have been professionally edited before and they have a reason for saying it.

I have no experience with local critique groups. I think they could be extremely helpful *if* people don't feel beholden to one another and can tell the truth kindly. If a too-negative or too-positive vibe is going on with a critique group, it's probably better to look for another group. "Critters" are there to save us from plunging in with a crummy story and to help us polish a good story.

Beta Readers: Betas are a handful of readers who are widely read in your specific genre. This can include authors or simply readers who (for example) "love mysteries," if you are writing a mystery. Betas read your book for inconsistencies in character, holes in plot, and elements that strike them the wrong way. Predictably, if you have 10-15 people doing this, you are going to get 10-15 opinions on various things to change with your book. It can totally wreck the direction of your story and make you forget which direction you were going in the first place.

This is why **I feel the optimal number of beta readers is three to five.** If two out of five readers of my genre comment on the same issue, I assume it needs work. If one comments on something but none of the others notice it, I usually think my reader pool at large won't notice it either. *But* I do consider every suggestion, and if I realize a change would make it stronger, I will make it.

Some authors send (leading) questions to the beta readers, questions such as, "Did you find that Jimmy seemed too weak in this scene?" I don't do that because I think it puts ideas into readers' heads and can taint their view of the book at large. I want *their* immediate impressions of things that stand out, for good or bad. So I send beta readers my e-book manuscript (I offer it in PDF, MOBI, or ePub format to give them e-reader options) and wait for them to respond. Then I integrate any rewrites based on my consideration of their observations.

You can utilize betas either before or after an editor, but it probably makes sense to use them first, in case you have to integrate major plot or character changes. Remember, **the primary purpose of betas is to make sure your novel will resonate with your target reader demographic before you publish**.

Editors: Paid editors can tackle various aspects of your polished draft:

Substantive Edits delve into the mechanics of your story: do the characters work? Does the plot have holes? You can also get *developmental edits,* which run along these lines but include more revisions and suggestions, etc.

Line Edits target your grammar, punctuation, sentence style, etc. *Proofreaders* can do much of this, alerting you to spelling errors, inconsistencies, and just a general overview.

The *first key* in hiring an editor is to **find an experienced one**. Don't trust testimonial blurbs—look at the books they have actually edited. That will tell you everything you need to know. Do you admire the writing? Does it read cleanly?

The *second key* in hiring an editor is to **find one you can work with**. Get a sample edit and see if the editor points out things you didn't notice before but suddenly see you need to change *because it will make your book stronger*. If you receive edits that don't seem to jibe with your book's purpose, gut your story, or don't look legitimate, you will want to shop around more. A good editor always makes you think, "Aha! Why didn't I see that?" A bad editor will make you think, "I can't do that and come out with the same book."

Please understand, this is assuming your manuscript *has already gone through critiquers' eyes*. This is assuming your story already holds water with readers. Editors polish that buffed-up draft into a gemstone.

Editorial costs vary wildly, but $1,500 is not unreasonable for a 75,000-word novel. So this is an expense you will have to keep in mind as you contemplate your editorial needs.

Early Readers: Early readers are a large pool of final-string readers. The purpose of early readers is:

- To land possible endorsers for your novel
- To build a core group that is ready to review your novel once it goes live
- To build buzz
- To catch small errors

What I give my early readers is my *near-final draft*. Edits and adjustments have been made. Cover art is attached (I want to give these readers a feel of the novel-to-come).

I treat this as a digital ARC (Advanced Reader Copy), similar to what traditional publishers distribute. I try to make sure it is available in PDF, MOBI, or ePub format so my readers can choose what works with their e-reader. You can easily convert Word files to e-reader files with programs like Calibre or Scrivener. Draft2Digital or Smashwords are also conversion options *if* you are using those sites to distribute your e-books. The cost of sending out softcovers at this stage is not only prohibitive, but it would bypass the final tweaks you will make after this early reader pool notices any stray spelling or punctuation errors.

As you can imagine, the larger the early reader pool, the better, especially for a debut novel. Fifty to sixty people would not be too many early readers for a debut. For most of my books, I shoot for the 35 range. It might seem like you're giving lots of books away for nothing, but you'll want those early reviews ready to be posted when your book goes live. Keep in mind that a good one third of your early reader pool may not ever review—more on that below.

Another strategy is to price your release at 99c for a limited time (perhaps for preorder and the first week's launch), so readers can pick it up cheaply and have it show up as a verified purchase.

Endorsements are something I would highly recommend for the debut author. They can jettison your debut from the "invisible" pile to the "must-read" pile because someone loves one of the authors who endorsed you and will now associate you with that author.

You want endorsers who are (a) excellent authors you respect, and (b) authors in your genre, if possible. Obviously this is especially true for non-fiction authors, who benefit greatly from the endorsements of experts in their field. For fiction authors, I think we have a bit more leeway. I find authors whose writing I respect and ask them if they would be my early readers. Often the answer is no (keep in mind authors are extremely busy!), but sometimes it's a yes. I might even procure an endorsement from an author who doesn't specifically write my genre, but enjoys something about my novel.

One thing I have learned: leave no stone unturned and write no one off. It doesn't hurt to approach authors who intimidate you—the worst that can happen is you can get rejected. And for many of us who have pursued traditional publishing before going indie, rejection is something we're well-acquainted with (sad to say).

Be sure to *give endorsers a target date for endorsements.* That way they know the window of time they have to read and work up a quote or two. And you can feature endorsements on your softcover book cover, front pages of your book, or in the Editorial Reviews section on Amazon or other vendors (on Amazon, you can't list them in Author Central until your book is live).

Early Reviews from your early readers are beneficial for a variety of reasons. For one, they can be posted on Goodreads before your book is available for purchase so people can read early impressions and add to their To-Read lists. They cannot be posted on Amazon until your book is live in the store.

Secondly, if you decide to run a freebie or special price on your book, some advertising sites won't list the novel unless you have a minimum number of reviews (more on this in Chapter Five).

The more reviews that go live along with your book, the more it looks like it's taking off. Sometimes winning a popularity contest is more about looking popular than actually *being* popular, to put it in totally shallow terms. In other words, if you look like a winner who's moving books, more people are going to notice you. Traditional publishing houses have understood this for a while and get ARCs out to various review sites, such as NetGalley or Publisher's Weekly, long before release date so reviews can pile up quickly post-release. Thankfully, indies can also adopt this policy and come out looking like champs.

Building Buzz is a marketing topic I will touch on later, but early readers are an important part of the process. If you have a core group of readers really jazzed about your novel, willing to spread the word the day it launches, you've already won half the battle.

Another thing: when you send out your ARCs, you will sit by your computer, waiting for early readers to contact you immediately about how they couldn't put your book down, how they love it, etc. Don't do this! Don't worry if you don't hear from them, even by the deadline. Just write it off.

I would say out of a pool of 40 early readers, you may get reviews from 25-30. Some will fall through the cracks, because (a) they didn't like your novel, and they don't know how to tell you this, (b) they won't read it till months post-release because they just don't have time, or (c) they totally forgot.

Don't ask anyone personally if they have read it yet. I've done this and it puts a major strain on your relationship and pressure on that reader. If you must follow up, do it by a group e-mail (I recommend setting up an early reader list on MailChimp or Mailerlite to save yourself from copying and pasting numerous e-mails), remind them of your release date, let them know reviews can go up now, etc. But once you nudge, back off and let it rest. I've had early readers review my book months after release. I'm just thankful when the reviews finally do come in!

Finally, early readers can **catch errors and typos** your critique partner or even editor has missed. There is a benefit to having many eyes on that manuscript before you hit *Publish*.

Chapter Three:
The Fun Part—Developing Cover Art and a Killer Blurb

At some point in the process you will want to conceptualize and develop **cover art**. Depending on the genre you're writing, you will need to have at least a basic concept of the storyline and a firm title and series title before working with a cover artist. I have had series covers designed before the books were written (to brand the series as a whole, and to take advantage of a bulk cover discount), so in those cases, I make sure I'm aligning my novel's descriptions with my cover.

One thing I cannot stress enough is this:

Cover art can make or break your book.

Indie authors do disagree on the importance of cover art, but the trend I see is that indies who are moving higher-priced indie books have eye-catching, professional-looking covers (and by "higher priced indie book," understand I mean $4.99-$6.99). When you launch your book on a site such as Amazon, it can quickly become invisible. One way to make sure it stands out and continues to garner interest is to nail your cover art.

In terms of cover art, you want something that would make *you* stop in your tracks if you saw it online or on the shelf at a bookstore (be ruthlessly honest with yourself here). Most authors' reader demographic looks a whole lot like themselves.

You should hire out cover art if you have very few graphic skills or if sample covers you've personally designed fail to garner an *immediate*, enthusiastic response from viewers (who are familiar with your genre). You really want to produce that "Wow" effect that hooks readers into checking out your book.

One way to find legitimate cover artists is to observe indie covers you love and find out who designed them. Often, indie groups share information like this. Joel Friedlander (The Book Designer) posts monthly cover art contests where you can see various genres represented. Or you can find someone talented with this sort of thing and barter services: if you're a skilled editor, and another author is a skilled cover designer, you can work out a trade.

Keep in mind, as with all four elements of indie

publishing, you might not have the budget to hire certain things out. You may have to pick and choose what's worth saving up for. For me, cover art and editing are the two elements I would not scrimp on. However, I was willing to learn the other two elements: formatting and marketing.

My first novel was published with practically no cost because my brother and critique partner helped me tremendously (my brother designed my cover and my critique partner formatted and uploaded my e-book). Part of being a savvy indie author is hunting down other options when you can't afford to hire out.

Covers can range in price from $200-$1,000 or more, depending on who does them. My brother worked with me on my first two covers, but because my mysteries will span an entire series (four or more books), we realized there weren't enough stock photos available of the model we chose for the initial cover for future books. Since designing covers isn't my brother's day job and he is now too busy, I have hired another cover designer for a redesign of that first mystery cover, aiming for a template we can easily use for all the covers in the series. This is another lovely perk of indie publishing: you can change covers at any time.

Before you begin cover design, be sure to check out

covers (traditionally or indie published) in your genre that jump out at you. There are elements that work in those covers and you'll want to integrate those. For example, a cozy mystery cover is often illustrated and light-hearted, versus a thriller cover that often uses heavier font and one graphic element. You need to understand what your genre readers *expect* and then be sure to have an eye-catching cover that still stands out from the rest. Tricky, but if you're working with a skilled cover designer, it is possible.

It's also easy to create Pinterest boards for cover art you'd like to emulate. I have secret Pinterest boards where I pin stock art I might use in my series; that way I can get a visual of the pictures altogether.

If you find it hard to be objective, throw a couple near-finalized sample covers out to your Facebook or blog readers (assuming you have worked on building a social media platform, as we discussed in the Introduction). Asking friends will only be effective if your friends *are willing to be honest* and *if they typically read in your genre*. An objective sampling is best—even in a Facebook group that reads your genre or an indie author group. There will usually be a majority opinion and I find the majority instinctively knows what will sell. Again, you're going for that "Wow" effect.

Another cheaper option is premade covers, but it can be tricky to find a premade that represents your individual story, and if you do find one, it's nearly impossible to find enough covers to keep an entire series looking consistent. I feel premades work best for standalone books (the cover of this book is a premade cover).

You also want a "Wow" effect with your **blurb**. There are many online posts about how to develop blurbs, but one thing you should try to do is **integrate keywords from your novel**. For instance, if it is a cozy mystery with a cupcake theme, be sure to include each of those words somehow in the blurb (*cozy, mystery, and cupcake*). When you categorize your book on Amazon and other sites, you can include all your keywords, but having them in the description (blurb) seems to help Amazon pull and match those words when placing your book in categories (honestly, no one really understands Amazon's algorithms regarding keywords/categories).

Another thing I recommend with your blurb is to **keep it short so it reads like the back cover copy** of a book (in fact, I do use my Amazon blurb as back cover copy on my softcovers). You want something that will intrigue and hook the reader, give them a sense of who the main character is, where the story is set, and give the reader an emotional *feeling* about the book.

When in doubt, ask your objective readers. I often throw one or two possible (honed) blurbs out to my Facebook followers, and sometimes I'm surprised to find I've given too much of my story away in the blurb. They help me narrow it down to what hooks them without spoiling the novel or confusing them with details.

Bottom line, both cover art and blurb (along with well-edited first sample chapters on Amazon) are what will sell your book. I have had reviewers pick up my indie novel, admitting they don't read indies, but they *had to* read it given the cover/blurb/first chapters. So a quality cover and blurb opens doors that might otherwise be shut. It sets you up for success right off the bat and presents your best face to the reader world. I know there have been instances when the cover alone has enticed me to buy a book. How about you?

(More on effective blurb-writing on the *Writer's Write* blog at http://writerswrite.co.za/how-to-write-an-irresistible-book-blurb-in-five-easy-steps.)

Chapter Four:
The Tedious Part—Formatting and Uploading your Book

Keep in mind that what may be tedious for me might be gravy to you. But proper formatting and uploading of your book is another crucial step in this process. As with all the four elements of indie publishing, you have two options here:

- **You can hire out your formatting**
- **You can learn to format**

If you're unfamiliar with formatting techniques, this can be the most tedious part of the process (it's the part that makes me want to run screaming from the computer). However, if you find a mentor who can teach you how to do it properly, you can get it done and it will become easier over time. With each book, your formatting skills will grow (I went back and reformatted my softcover after learning a few tricks such as full justification, etc.). I couldn't afford to hire it out the first time around, but I went to my critique partner, who knew what she was doing. She took time to visit (from across the country!) and showed me, step by step, how to format e-books. That old maxim "teach a man to fish, feed him for a life" kept coming to mind after her intense tutorial.

We've already touched on the conversion process in Chapter Two—using a program like Calibre or Scrivener to make your book accessible in PDF, MOBI, or ePub format for uploads to various sales sites.

Without going into too much mind-numbing detail, *e-readers use a different format than softcovers*. With softcover creation, you will have margins and fonts and section breaks that will look exactly like you want the book to look on the shelf. You will also need a wraparound book cover that includes spine design.

With e-book creation, you only need a front cover that meets the e-book specs. In the document itself, you will need to create bookmarks and hyperlinks (linking to each of your chapters—that's how e-readers jump from one place to another in the book).

Numerous indies have confirmed that the simpler your interior e-book design, the better. I tried fancy dingbat section breaks in one of mine, and wound up changing them multiple times before they finally showed up right on Kindle…and they *never* showed up correctly on Nook or Kobo. I decided then and there to use simple section breaks for my e-versions, such as *** or ~~~.

You will want to stick to a recognizable font like Times New Roman for your e-book. However, for your softcover, you can choose the font that works best with the tone of your novel, checking to make sure the font is embedded before you upload.

If your mind is swimming just thinking of formatting, uploading, or converting books, don't fear. Mine was too. Again, these things can be learned. But if you try to learn and don't come out with a competitive-looking, professional product, save up and outsource. Formatting and uploading is on the lower end of the pricing spectrum, averaging around $60-$100.

One caveat: before hiring a formatter, check their other books to see if they look comparable to traditional e-books (you compare easily with the sample chapters on Amazon). If the spacing is wonky or the fonts are strange, keep looking.

Finally, I strongly recommend ordering **proof copies** of your softcover before publishing it. You can see if you like the glossy or matte cover better, the ivory or white interior page color, and check if the wraparound cover fits your book properly. You will also need to check interior spacing and margins, not to mention do a read-aloud if you want that extra layer of error protection before publication.

Also, I recommend having your softcover ready to go when you publish your e-book. There will always be that reader who is excited when you launch your book, yet doesn't have an e-reader, and it's so much easier to have a link to the softcover you can share. In other words, it helps you maximize your readership. Some authors do choose to do e-books only. But with my novels, I like having the softcover option for readers and giveaways.

Whether to go with Amazon exclusively for your e-book or to branch out to other retailers is another discussion. I've tried both ways: Amazon *Select*, which is exclusive and allows for you to schedule freebies and countdowns, and Amazon *KDP*, which allows you to place the book on Nook, Kobo, iBooks, or other online retailers. Since Amazon is always in flux, you can keep up with the latest selling techniques via online forums or by following indie blogs. Suffice it to say, I adjust my strategies all the time and wouldn't ever say there is only one route to take.

The beauty of indie publishing is that it *is* so responsive to your readers. You learn by trial and error what price point works for your book (hint: price according to other indies in your genre). Indie publishing is a very organic process.

Chapter Five:
The Never-Ending Story— Marketing your Novel

First, please understand that your marketing started back when you began to develop a social media presence. Every other step above, from having your book thoroughly edited to choosing a smashing cover and blurb, is all part of the marketing process.

And here's why it's all marketing: you don't want to market a half-cooked book. Your readers will sense you aren't fully behind it. To be a passionate marketer, you have to believe one hundred percent that your book can compete with others in its genre. You have to know it's worth reading.

I say this because you *will* want to approach reviewers about your novel, and if the cover looks cheesy or the editing is slipshod, it's only going to succeed in making that reviewer reject you and even slam indie books in general. However, if your book looks like something they'd pick up in a library (and reads like that), those reviewers will be more open to reviewing indies in the future (yes, there is still a slight stigma against indie authors, but that diminishes every year as stellar indies hit the virtual and literal shelves).

Below, I'll give you some solid marketing steps that worked for me. Again—what worked for me (time-wise, in particular), may not work for you. I tend to be a relentless marketer. If I see my book is dropping in sales, I try to figure out ways to jack up the interest again (be it a 3-day freebie, finding new reviewers, etc.). So below are merely ideas for you to mull over. Use any or none of them. The best way to learn to market is to watch what your favorite authors and publishing houses do. Yes, they often have marketing firms behind them. But much of what traditionally published authors do, indie authors can do…and sometimes better.

One key advantage we have is that we *never* have to stop marketing our books. This is what is referred to as the "long tail" of indie publication. We are marketing over time as opposed to primarily focusing our marketing efforts on book launch month, which is the traditional approach.

The steps below are what I used to launch my debut novel. I tweaked them for my second novel, and nowadays, I focus on the readers I already have (in my Facebook reader groups and in my newsletters). In other words, I went big with the first novel and tried every marketing technique I could afford. With my following novels, I was able to choose what worked best and focus my efforts there.

Pre-publication Marketing Steps:

Build Buzz. For me, this involved:

- Having a **firm launch date**. I think this is most crucial for your *debut novel* and again, this is optional. After that, it's easy to simply announce a target publication month and then let readers know the minute your book is live. But for my first novel, I wanted that anticipation to build. I wanted a firm read-by date for early readers. I wanted it to feel like a traditionally published book (yes, I'll admit it). I even stayed up until midnight the day of release and had a midnight online launch party of sorts. I wouldn't have slept that night anyway!

- **Revealing my book cover** at least two months ahead of release and loading the book cover onto Goodreads, so people could add to their To-Read lists.

- Creating a series of **pinnable quotes** (on PicMonkey), along with a release date, so readers could get a flavor of my writing/setting/story and share the picture quotes ("memes") on Pinterest boards. Now, it's easy to share quotes on Instagram using various picture apps.

- Loading the first four chapters (or no more than 10% of your book if you're in Kindle Select) onto **Scribd** or onto your blog where people can easily access them. For added value for my newsletter subscribers, I make sure they receive the sample chapters before anyone else. Then the next day, I can blog the sample and share on social media sites. I know several people have bought my books based on those sample chapters alone.

This is also a wonderful time to **share your endorsements,** since they're often in those first pages of your book. Endorsements from authors in your genre can undeniably generate buzz. My readers tell me endorsements aren't as important when they know an author and are awaiting their next book. But they are so helpful for an unknown, debut author.

- Lining up a **blog tour**. For the first novel, I believe this is imperative. You never know which blogs will bring many book purchases your way, but more importantly, people who read in those circles will become familiar with your book and see it everywhere. Often, your early readers will also be authors or bloggers who are happy to share their review on their blogs. It is a lot of work to line up a blog tour, so I recommend asking for interview questions versus doing blog posts yourself. Otherwise, you get burned out fast talking about the same things over and over. Questions keep it shorter and shake it up a bit.

- Along these lines, offer **giveaways**. With your debut novel, I'm convinced you *cannot give away too many books*. The entire purpose of your debut novel is to reach as many new readers as you can. You can't do that if you're stingy with your book, waiting for people to find it. With a blog tour, I try to give away as many copies of my book as possible. One way to cut costs on this is to offer e-book copies. I tend to give Kindle gift copies of the book, which means I have to purchase them, but this benefits me three ways: (1) most readers know how to load from Amazon versus Smashwords or other venues, (2) I keep the royalties from that sale, and (3) my rank goes up on Amazon with my purchase. The only drawback is that reviews from Kindle-gifted books do not show up as verified reviews on Amazon.

- I ran a **reader photo campaign**. When I launched my first book, I created a themed photo campaign for my readers to participate in. Basically those photos are a very *loud* visual that says people are interested in reading your book. I still encourage readers to submit pictures anytime of themselves and my books and I maintain a Pinterest board dedicated to those pictures.

- I **vlogged.** This means I did a video recording on YouTube. In it, I talked about my book, or in the case of my debut, my critique partner interviewed me about various aspects of the soon-to-release novel. Not everyone feels comfortable vlogging, but it can be a great tool and can be uploaded to your Goodreads site, your blog, and elsewhere. I think vlogs help readers feel they are connecting with you personally.

- I did not do a **book trailer,** but that is something you can either learn to do or outsource, if you feel it will add to the visibility of your novel. For me, I don't usually watch book trailers, so I figured that wouldn't be where my readers would migrate, either. As I said above, our readers tend to look and act a whole lot like we do.

- You can submit your book to larger **review sites**, such as NetGalley. These sites require a fee, but you will definitely get reviews. I would just give the caveat that you need to make sure you choose a review site that targets readers in your genre and can guarantee a certain number of reviews.

Post-Publication Marketing Steps:

- Once your book is live on Amazon, you can develop your **Author Page** there (in Author Central). You can also load the endorsements in the Editorial Reviews section (you can't do this until your book is live).

- Run a **Goodreads giveaway** of at least three hard copies of your novel (Goodreads does *not* allow e-book giveaways). I recommend offering three books so you will (probably) reach at least one reader who will review. Keep in mind, Goodreads giveaways don't really target your reader demographic. Often people sign up hoping to win random free books, and they don't review it after they receive it. The benefit of Goodreads giveaways is that your book winds up on lots of To-Read lists and looks more popular. And as I said above, sometimes the person who *appears* the most popular *is* the most popular.

- Consider doing an **audio version** of your novel. You can easily do this via Amazon's ACX (Audible) program. You can either pay per hour or do a royalty share with the narrator. You also have the option of recording the book yourself, but you really need the right equipment to make sure it doesn't sound like an echo chamber, etc. Audiobooks are yet another way to get your book into readers' hands and increase visibility and accessibility, and according to 2017 predictions, they are only growing in popularity.

- Consider **price drops or freebies** (but only after you have 20 or more reviews to list with freebie advertisement sites). Every author has to wrestle with their book's price point and pricing strategy. Some authors don't believe in doing freebies, and I totally respect that. For me, it was a valuable marketing tool. In three days, I had 11,000 downloads of my historical novel. Out of those 11,000 downloads, I might have had about thirty reviews trickle in on Amazon.

However, the thing to keep in mind is that **not all readers who love your book will review it on**

Amazon. A freebie extends your reach farther than you might imagine. Years later, I have talked to people who loved my book but never reviewed it. The risk with going free is that you will net some low-star reviews from people who didn't read the sample, don't normally read in your genre, etc. But the benefits far outweigh the risks for me because my book will reach some soon-to-be-loyal readers I couldn't have reached any other way.

If you do go free, be sure to give yourself a couple of months ahead of time so you can list your book with freebie advertising sites. As I mentioned above, you will need 20 or more reviews to list with most sites. **Bookbub** is, hands-down, the most beneficial site, as it targets books to their readership. However, it is very expensive. **E-Reader News Today** (ENT) and **Robin Reads** are ad sites that are far cheaper, but still effective. The aforementioned ad sites are quite selective and require a minimum number of reviews, and this is where a great cover and blurb can go a long way. There are also numerous sites that will list free books for free. It takes time and research to compile your list of go-to advertisement sites for your freebies.

Another strategy is going "**permafree**" (permanently free, often across many e-book platforms) with one of your books. I have used this strategy with only two books in a series and it tripled my income on the second book alone.

But please note, the permafree strategy *only* works to generate income if you use it for book one in a series or for standalone books in the same genre, because it acts as a funnel to pull readers in and make them buy the next book(s). Which brings me to the final, and most important marketing step…

- Write the next book! These days, many indies write at least three books in a series before publishing the first one, and that's a wise plan. I didn't do that, and instead wrote and published books in two different genres (historical and contemporary mystery). Now I have readers in both genres and I'm scrambling to get more books out in both series. If you can get ahead of the curve and have many books in the queue before publishing, it will help you. If not, just know you need to immediately start writing the next book post-publication because loyal readers are (thankfully) a hungry lot!

You will hear this mantra in most indie forums: *The best marketing is the next book*. And it's true. Even if your debut novel is a masterpiece and well-received, the more books you have out, the more income you will make.

I like having the indie author freedom to genre-hop, but I am at the point in my writing career where I see the benefit of building on your fan base and writing more books, either in the same genre or the same series.

Wrap-Up and My Author Biography

I hope this little handbook has given you a good idea of what you're getting into when you decide to indie publish. I'll give you a little of my own back story, in case you're wondering why I'm writing this book.

My own road to indie publication veered from the traditional publishing path I had pursued for about six years. In those six years, I had three agents and submitted three novels to publishing houses only to be rejected for various reasons (my first novel was too short, my second not considered a marketable time period, etc.).

However, with indie publishing, I was able to take that "unmarketable" Viking book and hit my niche market square on. My Viking historical, *God's*

Daughter, has been on the Amazon Norse Best-Seller list for four years.

My debut launch exceeded my expectations. I went into this gig with low expectations, telling myself if I made $200 off my debut Viking novel, I would be pleased. That debut novel allowed me to fund a family vacation that would have otherwise been impossible.

As of mid-2017, I have published six books (you can find all my books at http://heatherdaygilbert.com/my-novels/), and I have two more slated for release later this year. I have received a starred *Publisher's Weekly* review on my second Viking historical, *Forest Child*. I have received a Grace Award for my second mystery, *Trial by Twelve*. I've launched a 3-book series in yet another genre—romantic suspense. And I have an agent working with me as we pursue a movie option on one of my novels. I say these things not to brag, but to encourage you if you're on the fence, wondering if indie publishing is too great a risk. My awards and opportunities would not have come about had I simply waited for that first book to get picked up by a traditional publisher, because I might still be waiting.

I look at indie publishing as a great adventure. Yes, it is a lot to handle, and sometimes I wish I could go back to simply *writing*, not managing all the other aspects of my books' success. Therefore, I am still pursuing traditional publishing opportunities, and in fact I have already been traditionally published (*The Message in a Bottle Romance Collection*), so I am actually classified as a "hybrid author," not a strict indie.

With my indie books, I appreciate the control I have over my books' presentation, the immediate access I have to my sales reports, and the freedom to personally price and market my work. I love the freedom of choosing the narrator whose voice fits my audiobooks, instead of having one assigned to me by a publishing house. I don't have to split profits with agents, publishing houses, etc.

Indie publishing isn't something that should be entered into lightly. Yes, many things can be learned on the job. But you want to take time to weigh your approach to your indie career *before* you launch it, because you will be your own career manager. Even if you have an agent, most agents aren't up-to-date with indie publishing, simply because methods change all the time (as do the Amazon rules!), and that is not an agent's job. It is *our* job as indie authors to stay plugged into the industry, and the best way to do that is through talking with other indies and following indie blogs.

I wish you all the best if you choose to indie publish.

Please feel free to contact me at heatherdaygilbert (at) gmail (dot) com with questions.

You can find me at heatherdaygilbert.com. Sign up for my Author Newsletter at http://eepurl.com/Q6w6X.

READ ON for a bonus chapter!

Bonus: Wise Words from Multi-Published Indie Authors

In this value-added section, seasoned indie authors offer their words of wisdom…things they have often learned the hard way. As you can see, we all take different approaches to the four key elements of indie publishing. Doubtless, some of these will resonate with you as you consider becoming an independent publisher. Please click the authors' names, which link directly to their websites. These authors are an outstanding representation of indie publishing in both non-fiction and fiction genres.

"Only begin your marketing phase when you have something for people to buy, by which I mean more than one book. This usually means 3 to 5 books. Because people aren't buying your marketing prose—Facebook posts, blog entries, ads, and so forth. The best advertising for your book is the next book." ~**Shelley Adina**, RITA Award winner and Christy finalist

"Being successful requires good writing, good covers, good editing, and good marketing. There's also a touch of luck in there, because you can do all of the right things and have a great book, but still not find an audience. The key is to keep growing, keep improving, and keep writing. Listen to feedback, never think you've fully arrived no matter what your success, and learn from those who've gone before you." ~**Christy Barritt**, Award-Winning Author

"You don't have to get everything perfect the first time. Allow yourself the freedom to do what you can now, and improve what you can and want to later after you gain more experience." ~**Lynnette Bonner**, multi-published author

"My second piece of advice to new authors would be not to rush into publishing. Take the time to really learn your craft. Read a ton, especially in your genre. And study, study, study the craft." ~**Lynnette Bonner**, multi-published author

"If you're going to indie-publish, make a production plan for yourself. Even if you outsource things like editing and cover art, you are still the "producer." You produce the written words, you produce the edits and formatting, you produce the cover art, you produce the digital book, you produce the print copy. Plan on writing and publishing at least one book a year *minimum*. If that feels like too much, don't stress about publishing your first book until you have a second one well on its way to "The End." Put your time and energy into writing that next book." ~**Becky Doughty**, author of the bestselling *Elderberry Croft* series

"I am terrible about marketing. I prefer to pay people to market for me. So I've learned to self-edit, format, and create solid covers myself so I can use my few dollars on marketing. This is the beauty of self-publishing—we get to determine who does what…and then we can change our minds if it isn't working for us!" ~**Becky Doughty**, author of the bestselling *Elderberry Croft* series

"Joining in group collections with other authors of the same skill level, whether you are using a new story or the first in a series, is one of the best marketing tools available. Then, you have a group marketing and reach a larger audience." ~**Cynthia Hickey**, author of the best selling *Nosy Neighbor* cozy mystery series—an Amazon #1 Bestseller for four months straight

"Know what you know, and make it your life's goal to learn what you don't yet know. In between times: pay someone to do what you can't yet do. Then, at the end of a long, happy career, you will have a library of great books and a life you spent learning, collaborating and creating." ~**Traci Hilton,** Amazon Bestselling Religious Fiction Author

"Quality, quantity, and series—deliver all three and, oh, the possibilities!" ~**Tamara Leigh**, USA Today Bestselling Author

"At the back of your book, always include 'If you loved the book, you can join here to sign up for more' so that people can join your list, but also ask nicely for a review if they loved the book, with a direct link to the sales page so that they can review it instantly." ~**Joanna Penn**, NYT and USA Today Bestselling Thriller Author (quote used with permission from Joanna's *How to Market a Book*)

"Having a brand doesn't mean that you need an expensive logo or unique design (although you can do these things). It means that you have an image and words associated with you in people's minds." ~**Joanna**

Penn, NYT and USA Today Bestselling Thriller Author (quote used with permission from Joanna's *How to Market a Book*)

"If you don't take your writing seriously, no one else will either. This is particularly valuable in combating the guilt we occasionally feel for taking the time to make writing a priority. But once you realize you are the only one who can make it a priority, it's easier to get serious and start making it clear (as tactfully as possible) to others that your writing time is not to be taken lightly." ~**K.M. Weiland**, IPPY and NIEA Award-winning, internationally published Bestselling author

ACKNOWLEDGMENTS

I want to thank those who have pushed me forward, even when I was unsure I was ready to step out and go indie. I'm so thankful for your belief in my writing.

Special thanks for the proofreading services of my author friend, Jan Thompson, on this handbook. And thanks for the blurb input from another author friend, Mirtika Schultz, whom I have henceforth dubbed "The Blurb Whisperer." Also, thank you to my friend, über-editor Andy Scheer, for making time to read this.

Thank you also to my beta readers, my endorsers, and to the experienced authors who submitted their wise, helpful quotes for upcoming indie authors. I'm so glad we can learn from each other.

Finally, thank *you* for reading this book and I hope you take away many helpful ideas as you consider following the indie publishing dream. If you found it helpful, please share with your author friends and be sure to review it on Amazon and Goodreads.

And please sign up for my author newsletter at http://eepurl.com/Q6w6X, so you can keep up with my upcoming specials and releases.

www.ingramcontent.com/pod-product-compliance
Lightning Source LLC
Chambersburg PA
CBHW031546210526
45464CB00003B/1167